Wild Animals

By Cameron Macintosh

This wild colt is free!

No one can ride it.

This man can’t wind a rope around the colt.

It will bolt from him!

This is a wild hog.

A hog is a kind of pig.

Wild hogs love to lie in the mud.

The mud is cold, but they don't mind!

You can't walk a wild dog on a leash!

This dog runs around with its family behind it.

Wild dogs are bold.

If they find a wild hog,
they might fight it!

Most wild bats love to snack on bugs.

They also like to find fruit and chew the rind.

This is a wild fox.

Its child is called a kit.
Wild foxes are kind
to their kits.

When it gets cold,
this fox makes its fur white.
It blends into the snow.

It looks different!

Wild owls hunt at night.

They are not blind in the dark.
They see very well!

This owl folds its wings to nap on an old post.

This possum holds on by winding its tail around a branch.

You can spot possums in the wild or in your backyard!

CHECKING FOR MEANING

1. Why can't the man catch the wild colt with a rope? *(Literal)*
2. What does a wild hog love to do? *(Literal)*
3. Do you think wild dogs and wild hogs like each other? Why? *(Inferential)*
4. Which animal do you think is the most wild? Why? *(Evaluative)*

EXTENDING VOCABULARY

bold	Why is the wild dog described as *bold* in the text? What is another word with a similar meaning to *bold*?
blends	Read the word *blends*. What does it mean if the fox's fur blends into the snow? Is it easy or hard to see the fox against the snow?
backyard	Read the word *backyard*. What two smaller words make up this word? Does your home have a backyard? What are some other animals you might see in your backyard?

MOVING BEYOND THE TEXT

1. What wild animals might you see near where you live?
2. What is your favourite wild animal? Why?
3. What should you do if you see a wild animal?
4. When have you felt bold? What were you doing?

TIME TO WRITE

Write about your favourite wild animal. Include what it looks like and where you can see it.